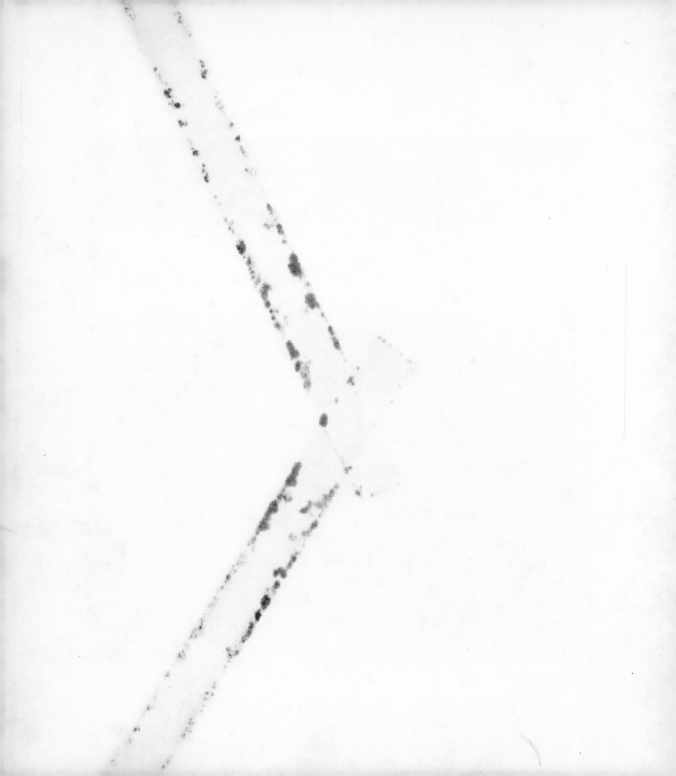

SCIENCE GAMES

Laurence B. White, Jr.

drawings by

Marc Tolon Brown

Addison-Wesley

Books by Laurence B. White, Jr.

Science Games
Science Puzzles
Science Toys
Science Tricks
Investigating Science with Coins
Investigating Science with Nails
Investigating Science with Paper
Investigating Science with Rubber Bands
So You Want to be a Magician?

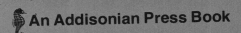 **An Addisonian Press Book**

To Dave . . .
who guarantees every experiment
because they worked for him

Text Copyright © 1975 by Laurence B. White, Jr.
Illustrations Copyright ©1975 by Marc Tolon Brown
All Rights Reserved
Addison-Wesley Publishing Company, Inc.
Reading, Massachusetts 01867
Printed in the United States of America
First Printing

HA/WZ   08600   3/75

Library of Congress Cataloging in Publication Data

White, Laurence B
  Science games.

  SUMMARY: Simple games and experiments which
demonstrate basic scientific principles.
  "An Addisonian Press book."
  1. Science—Experiments—Juvenile literature.
[1. Science—Experiments.   2.   Scientific recreations]
I. Brown, Marc Tolon, illus.   II.   Title.
Q163.W488   507'.2   74-2137
ISBN 0-201-08600-X

Games are to Play

A game is a challenge.
Something to try . . . something to learn . . .
something to be good at.

- Race a drop of water
- Blow the biggest bubble
- Build an eight cup skyscraper

The games in this book work with science!
Science, like a game, is something to try . . .
to learn . . . and be good at.
What a nice way to investigate science . . .
to play science games . . .
by yourself, with friends,
and even with your cat!

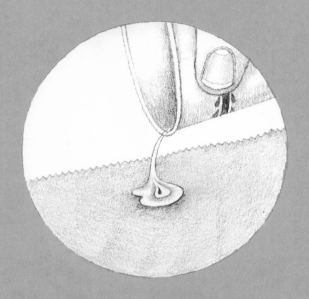

Race with a Drop of Water

Get a big piece of waxed paper.
Lay it flat.
Pour a little water on it.
The water will form a big round drop.
Pick up the paper carefully.
Hold it by both ends.
Tip the paper back and forth.
Make the water drop run around.
How fast can you make it go?
Watch it . . . you may tip a bit too far!

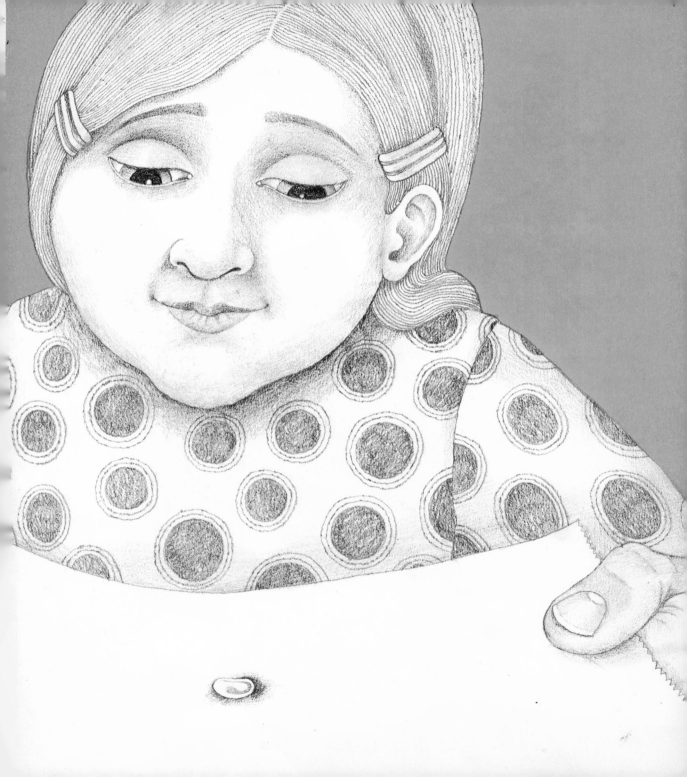

Shadow Game

What is this a shadow of? A dog?
No, it just looks like a dog.
The shadow was really made by a hand.
Shadows are made by blocking out light.
They really are nothing, but they can look like something.
Hold your hands in the sunlight,
or hold your hands between a lamp and a wall.
Can you make shadows that look like these?

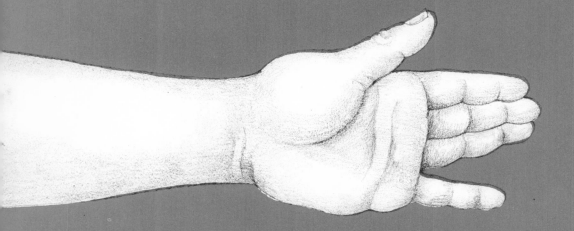

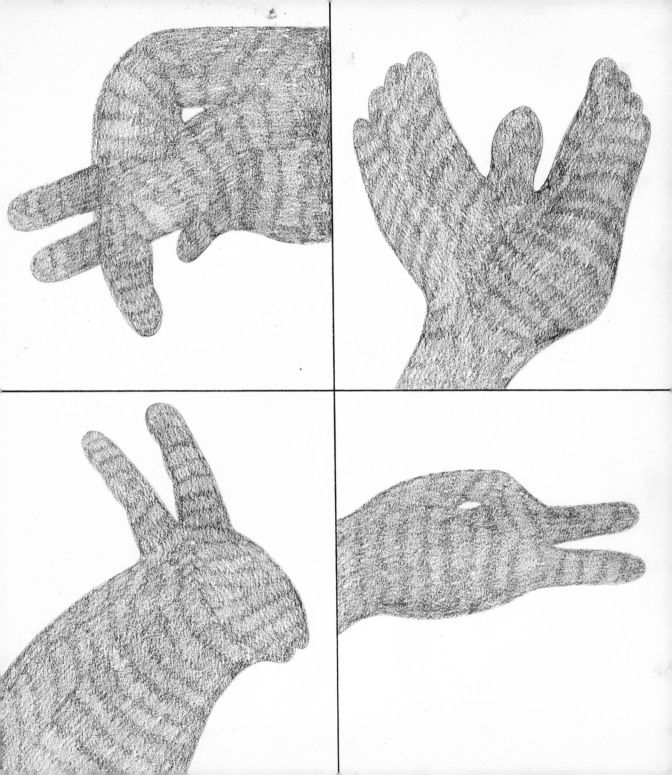

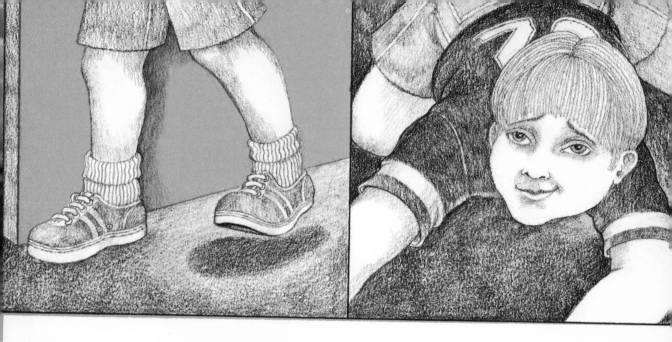

Stand Up, Do Not Fall Down

Sometimes you cannot keep from falling.
Try this. Stand sideways against a wall.
Push the side of your foot against the wall.
Now try to lift your other foot.
It feels like it is stuck to the floor.
The wall stops your body from bending.
If you did lift your foot,
without bending your body,
you would fall down!

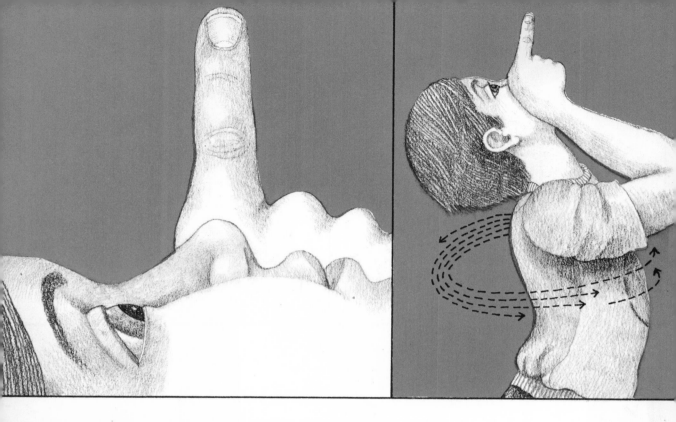

Can You Walk in a Straight Line?

Look up.

Point your finger up from the end of your nose.

Look at the end of your finger.

Keep looking and turn around three times.

Then walk in a straight line.

You try to walk straight,

but you still feel like you are going around.

It will make you very dizzy.

Can You Blow 100 Bubbles?

Can you blow 100 bubbles?

With one breath?

Pour some dishwashing liquid in a cup.

Dip in one end of a drinking straw.

Take it out.

Blow in the other end.

Keep blowing.

You will blow lots of bubbles.

The bubbles will be tiny.

You may even blow 100.

Blow the Biggest Bubble

Who can blow the biggest bubble?
Give everyone a drinking straw.
Use dishwashing liquid for soap.
Dip in the straw and blow gently.
Who blows the biggest bubble?
Try cutting your straw end like a cross.
Now it will hold more soap.
Your bubble will be the biggest.

How High Can You Float a Bubble?

Try this in the winter on a very cold day.
Go outdoors with some bubble soap.
Blow some bubbles.
Your warm breath makes the bubbles very light.
They are much lighter than the cold winter air.
The bubbles will quickly float upwards.
How high?

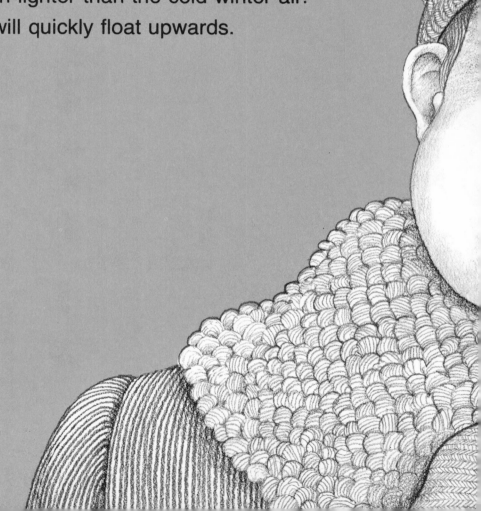

Pencil Pick Up

Lay a pencil in the middle of a table.

Bend down. Look at the pencil level with the tabletop.

Close one eye. Keep it closed.

Quickly reach out and try to pick up the pencil.

You will probably miss it.

It is very hard to do.

Now try it with both eyes open.

It is easy with two eyes helping.

How Hot Can You Make It?

Push a thumbtack into a pencil eraser.
Touch the thumbtack with your lip.
It feels cool.
Rub the tack hard on your sleeve.
Rub hard 20 times.
Touch it to your lips.
It feels warm.
Rubbing makes it hot . . .
The harder you rub . . .
The longer you rub . . .
How hot can you make the thumbtack?

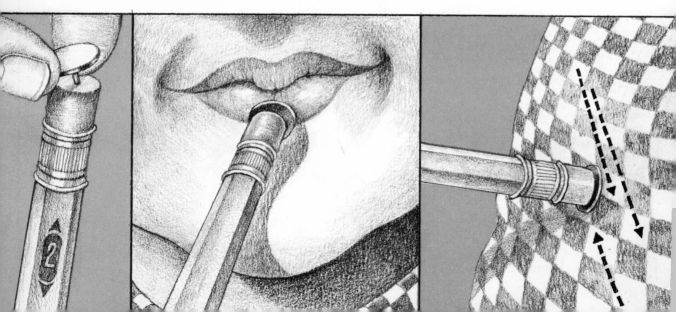

Do Two Things Together

Can you do two things at the same time?
Most people cannot.
Print your name on a piece of paper.
Move your foot in a circle.
Try to do both at the same time.
Why is it hard to do?
Because you have to think
about your hand and foot
doing different things.

How Cold Can You Make It?

Soak a facecloth in warm water.
Quickly . . . take it outdoors.
Hold it by one corner.
Spin it around and count to ten.
Touch your face with the cloth.
Surprise! It is very cool.
Spinning dries some of the water.
As the water dries, the cloth gets cooler.

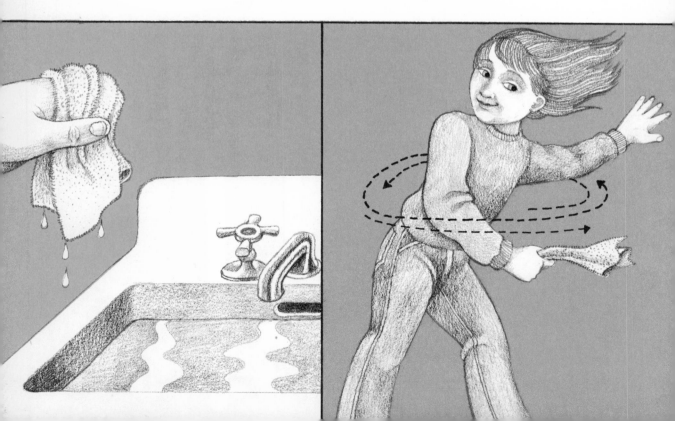

Are You As Long As Your Arms?

Hold your arms and hands out straight.

Have someone cut a string just that long.

Put one end of the string on the floor.

Does the other end reach the top of your head?

Try it with other people.

Are most people as tall as their arms are long?

Penny Dropping

Drop some coins into an empty glass.
Will they always fall into the glass?
Pretty easy, wasn't it?
But, what happens if you put the glass at
the bottom of a bowl of water?
Water slows the coins down.
It pushes the coins aside.
A lot of them miss the glass.

Drink Some Raindrops

Next time it rains
set an empty glass outside.
Catch some raindrops in it.
Raindrops are pure water.
You can drink raindrops.
The water may taste strange.
Most water we drink comes from the ground.

Touch Your Fingers

Hold your arms out straight and
point your fingers.
Then close your eyes.
Try to touch your fingers together.
You can do it if you go slowly.
If you move faster it gets harder.
Now open your eyes and try it.
Much easier, isn't it? Why?
Because our eyes help show
our bodies how to move.

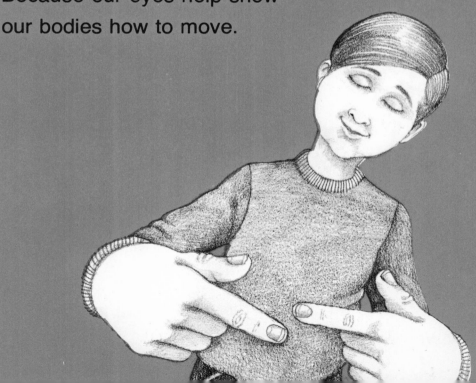

Breathe and Swallow

Breathe through your nose.
Now try to swallow.
Can you do them both
at the same time?
You cannot.
Nobody can.
Your nose and throat are connected
by a little tube in your head.
When you breathe you cannot swallow.
When you swallow you cannot breathe.

Printing Your Name

Can you print your own name?
That's easy!
But sometimes it is very hard.
Look in a mirror.
Try printing your name
while you look in the mirror.
A mirror turns things around.
Try it and you will see!

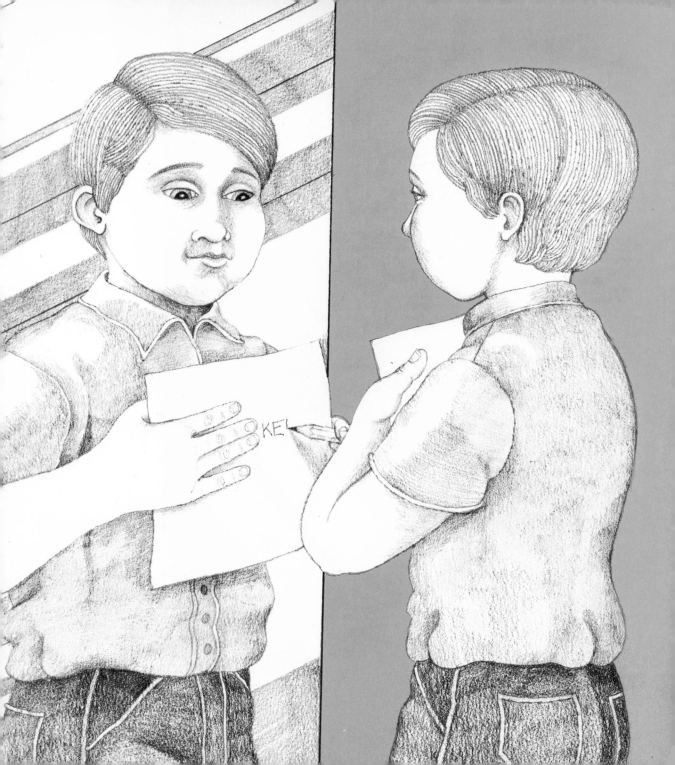

The Blink Game

Roll a sheet of paper into a big ball.
Have a friend look out a window.
You stand on the other side of the window.
Toss the paper ball at his face.
The glass will stop the paper,
but your friend will blink.
Have your friend try it with you.
It is very hard not to blink
no matter how many times you try.

Can You Blow the Ball Out?

Roll a little piece of aluminum foil in a ball.
Drop it in a funnel.
Ask friends to try to blow it out.
They cannot do it.
Their wind goes around the ball,
and out the bottom of the funnel.
Now you blow.
(But, first put your finger over the bottom.)
Now you can blow the ball out.

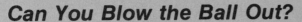

You Can Win This Balance Game

Try to balance a ruler on one finger.

Ask your friends to try too.

It is hard to do.

Who can balance it the longest?

You can!

Try this trick.

Stick a ball of clay on the top of the ruler.

Now try to balance it.

It is much easier now.

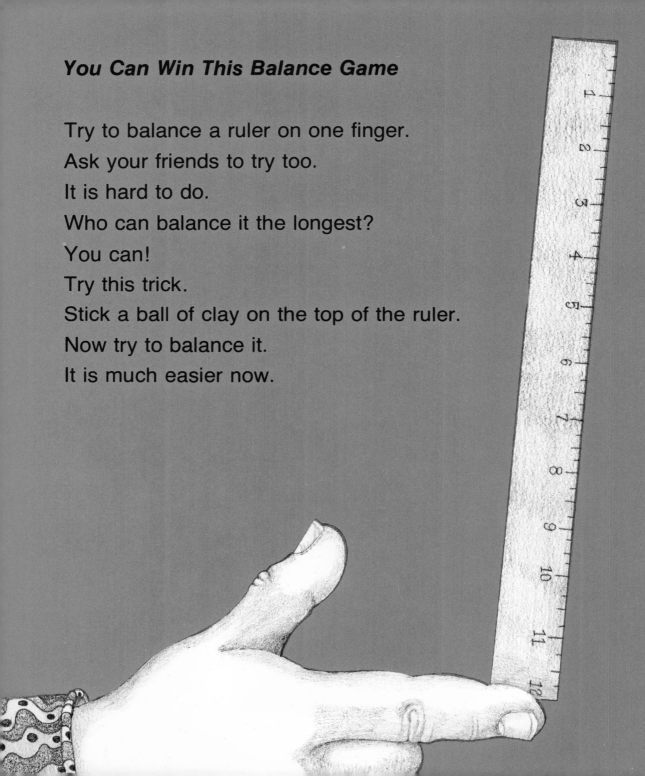

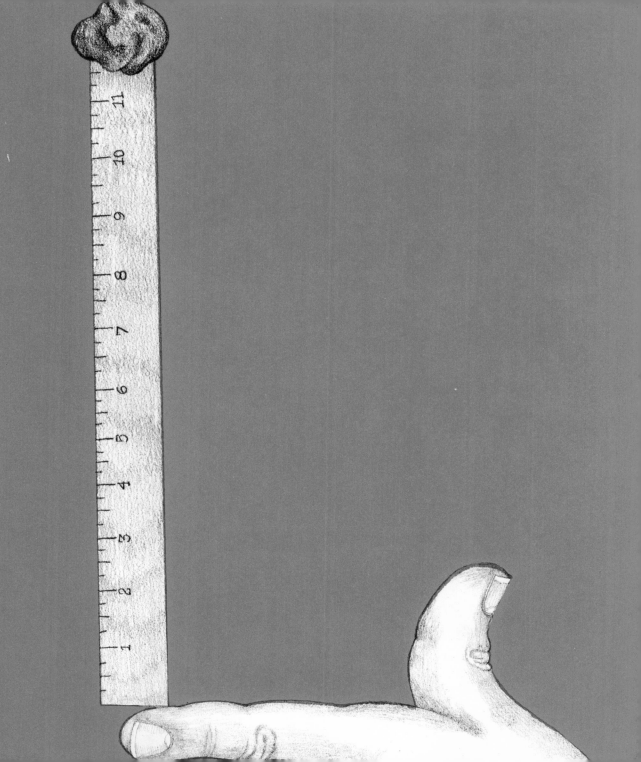

Send Secret Signals

Want to send secret signals to a friend?
And make sure others don't hear the signals?
Have your friend lay his head on a table.
Put your hand under the table.
Tap softly on the bottom of the tabletop.
The sound will travel through the table.
Your friend will hear your secret taps.
But only your friend.
No one else will. Why not?

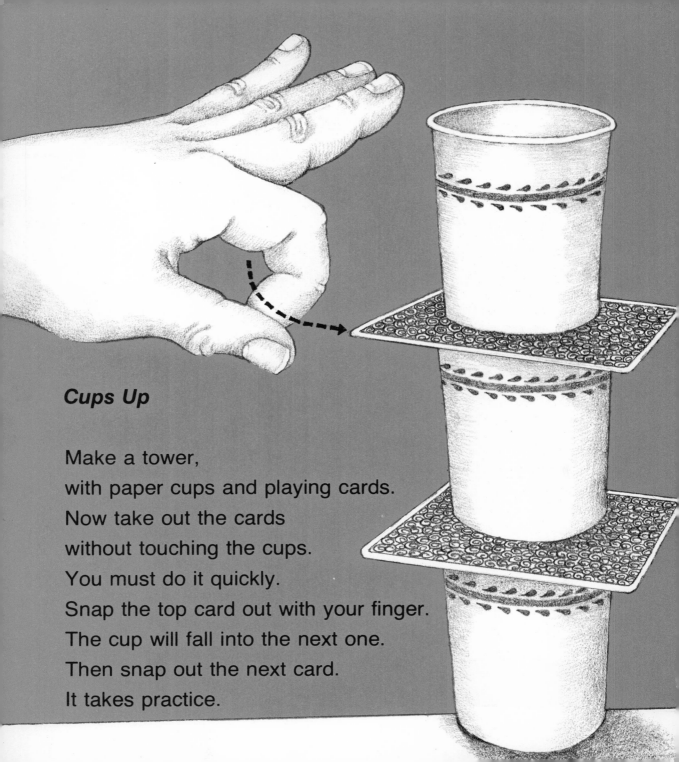

Cups Up

Make a tower,
with paper cups and playing cards.
Now take out the cards
without touching the cups.
You must do it quickly.
Snap the top card out with your finger.
The cup will fall into the next one.
Then snap out the next card.
It takes practice.

Build a Skyscraper

A skyscraper is a tall skinny building.
How high can you build one?
Make it out of paper cups.
Stack them up and down.
The higher . . . the harder!
(I made one eight cups high.)
You cannot make one as tall as a real skyscraper.
But then real skyscrapers are harder to build.

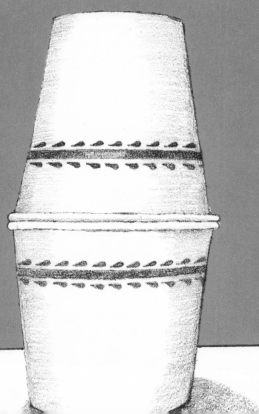

Who Has the Most Teeth?

Count teeth.
Count yours, your friends.'
Babies do not have any teeth at all.
Grown-ups usually have 32 teeth.
You get more teeth as you grow older.
So . . . if you find people with more than you,
do not worry. You will catch up!

Is Your Cat Right or Left Pawed?

Some people are right handed.
Some people are left handed.
Which are you?
Which is your cat?
Play a game with your cat and find out.
Put some food in a tall jar.
Put it near your cat.
Which paw does he use to get it out.
Try again.
Does he always use the same paw?

The games in this book work with science.
Like a game, science is something
to try . . .
to learn . . .
and to be good at.
Keep playing these games.

You will get better . . .
And you will understand
more why the games work.
What a nice way
to investigate science.

DATE DUE

Hodge					
Henson					

DEMCO 38-301

White   75-203